COLONIAL

TRADITIONS

Verna Fisher

Nomad Press
A division of Nomad Communications
10 9 8 7 6 5 4 3 2 1
Copyright © 2011 by Nomad Press.
All rights reserved.

This book was manufactured by
Regal Printing Limited in China
June 2011, Job #1105033
ISBN: 978-1-936313-63-1

Illustrations by Andrew Christensen
Educational Consultant, Marla Conn

Questions regarding the ordering of this book should be addressed to
Independent Publishers Group
814 N. Franklin St.
Chicago, IL 60610
www.ipgbook.com

Nomad Press
2456 Christian St.
White River Junction, VT 05001
www.nomadpress.net

Contents

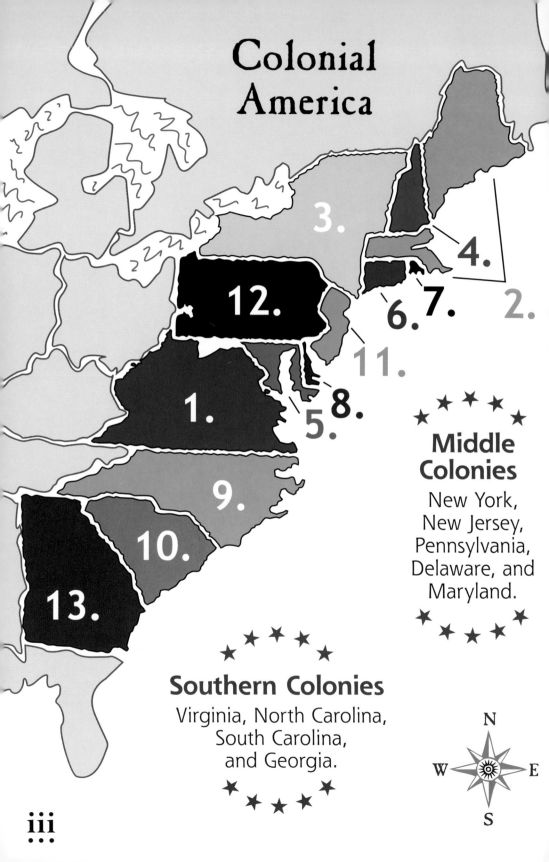

Colonial America

3.

12.

4.

6.
7.
2.

11.

1.
5.
8.

9.

10.

13.

Middle Colonies
New York,
New Jersey,
Pennsylvania,
Delaware, and
Maryland.

Southern Colonies
Virginia, North Carolina,
South Carolina,
and Georgia.

N
W E
S

New England

Massachusetts,
New Hampshire, Connecticut,
and Rhode Island.

In the 1600s, people began leaving Europe to settle in America. Some were explorers searching for gold, while others came looking for freedom.

Jamestown in Virginia and Plymouth in Massachusetts were two of the earliest settlements where these people came to start a new life.

1607

1. Virginia
2. Massachusetts
3. New York
4. New Hampshire
5. Maryland
6. Connecticut
7. Rhode Island
8. Delaware
9. North Carolina
10. South Carolina
11. New Jersey
12. Pennsylvania
13. Georgia

1733

Making Work Fun

When the **colonists** first settled the **New World**, they had to do everything by hand. They did not have electricity or machines. The colonists grew their own food and sewed their own clothes. They built their own homes and barns.

Words to Know

Even though the colonists worked very
hard, they found ways to add some fun to
their lives. Colonists created **traditions**
around work events and holidays. This
made work more enjoyable. It gave
everyone something to look forward to.

Neighbors Helping Neighbors

Difficult work became **community** events that involved neighbors helping each other. One of the most common work traditions on a colonial farm was a **barn raising**.

community: a group of people living in an area together.

barn raising: building a wooden barn with a group of people.

Words to Know

Everyone in the community was expected to help with a barn raising.

A barn was an important building during colonial times. It was used to store hay and keep animals. But building a barn was a huge job, too big for one family to build alone.

post: a strong piece of wood stood straight up for support.

beam: a strong piece of wood laid across posts for support.

bonds: links between people.

Words to Know

First the farmer cut **posts** and **beams** for the barn out of wood from trees. Then as many as 100 men gathered to work. They built the frames for the walls out of the posts and beams. The men used ropes and poles to raise the frames up into place, all in one day.

The women cooked while the men worked on the barn. The children helped, too. Afterward everyone shared in some fun by eating, dancing, and relaxing together. It was a celebration that strengthened the **bonds** in the community.

Did You Know?

The Amish people of Pennsylvania and Ohio still have barn raisings today.

"Aw, Shucks"

Many jobs were more fun to do in a group. A **cornhusking** was held to peel the ears of corn from an entire fall **harvest**. On a cool fall evening the barn was cleared and decorated for a **frolic**.

Words to Know

The group sat in a circle, working together to peel the corn. The colonists talked and enjoyed each other's company. Meanwhile the peeled ears of corn piled up in the center of the circle. When their work was done it was time for a party with food, drinks, music, and dancing.

Cornhusking was called "shucking" in the Southern Colonies.

Just For Girls

A quilting bee was a work frolic for women and girls. They gathered to make a quilt. Quilts are large, cozy blankets made of lots of fabric pieces sewn together.

In colonial times quilts were sewn together by hand. Women and girls were very proud of their tiny, even stitches.

Today you can buy quilts in a store. Most quilters use a sewing machine.

Women helped each other make beautiful quilts for their homes. It was a chance for the women to finish a large task together. The younger girls watched and helped out as part of their training.

recycle: to use something again.

wadding: a layer of wool or cotton stuffing. It gives a quilt thickness and warmth.

Words to Know

Quilting bees were planned like the other work frolics. The lady asking for help did a lot of the work before the event. She cut the pieces of fabric and sewed them together in beautiful patterns for the quilt top. Some of the patterns had fun names like Bear's Paw, Pinwheel, and Log Cabin.

Pinwheel

Bear's Paw

Log Cabin

Cloth from old clothes and blankets was often **recycled** into pieces for a quilt.

At the quilting bee the women laid down a sheet of plain cloth, and covered it with the layer of **wadding**. The quilt top went over the wadding. Then the women sewed all the layers together. Their stitching could be very fancy! Food and fun came after the work was finished.

Let's Celebrate the Harvest!

In 1621, the **Pilgrims** celebrated their good harvest with a three-day feast. They gave thanks to the Native Americans for teaching them how to grow corn and hunt.

Thanksgiving became an official American holiday in 1863.

The **Wampanoag** brought five deer to the celebration, while the Pilgrims cooked many turkeys and geese. The meal also included fish, clams, corn, carrots, and onions. Our Thanksgiving is based on this first harvest feast.

Puritans: a group of colonists that lived a simple life. Their religion was very strict.

fine: money owed for breaking a law.

united: joined with others.

Words to Know

At first only some of the colonies celebrated Christmas. In many New England communities, celebrating Christmas was forbidden by the **Puritan** religion. In Massachusetts and Connecticut, anyone caught celebrating the holiday had to pay a **fine**.

In the Middle Colonies, Christmas was a holiday frolic for adults only, with food, singing, and dancing. Children were not part of the celebration.

CELEBRATION OF CHRISTMAS IS FORBIDDE

Did You Know?

Early settlers celebrated birthdays of kings or queens from their homelands. When settlers felt more **united** as a group of Americans, these celebrations stopped.

Name That Tune

Many families in **Colonial America** played music and sang songs. Music was important to work and holiday frolics. It was enjoyed in the evening after a long day.

The most common instruments were the banjo, flute, and fiddle. These instruments were played mostly by men. Women played the **harpsichord**.

Colonial America: the name given to this country when talking about the years 1607–1776.

harpsichord: an instrument similar to a piano. It had an upper and lower keyboard.

hymns: songs written for praise or prayer.

Words to Know

The colonists sang songs from their homelands. Different regions became known for certain types of music. Church **hymns** were popular in the New England Colonies, because the Puritan people were very religious.

In the Middle Colonies, there were settlers from Scotland, Ireland, Germany, Holland, France, and England. They brought instruments and music from their different **cultures**. These included organs, bagpipes, and fiddle tunes.

The Southern colonists enjoyed church music as well as non-church music. They went to concerts, **balls**, and music clubs. Some **plantation** owners gave their **slaves** instruments so they could play music for plantation balls.

Words to Know

Slaves brought their own music with them from Africa. They sang while they worked in the fields and in their free time. Their songs were about their faith and the struggles in their hard lives.

Slave owners wanted their slaves to sing as they worked so that they would work harder. But they wanted the songs to have a cheerful tune, even if the words were not about happy things.

Did You Know?

Colonial slaves were not allowed to play drums. Slave owners feared they would use drums to **communicate** about their working conditions and disobey their owners.

The songs the slaves sang were rich in passion and later influenced blues and gospel music.

Tell Me A Story

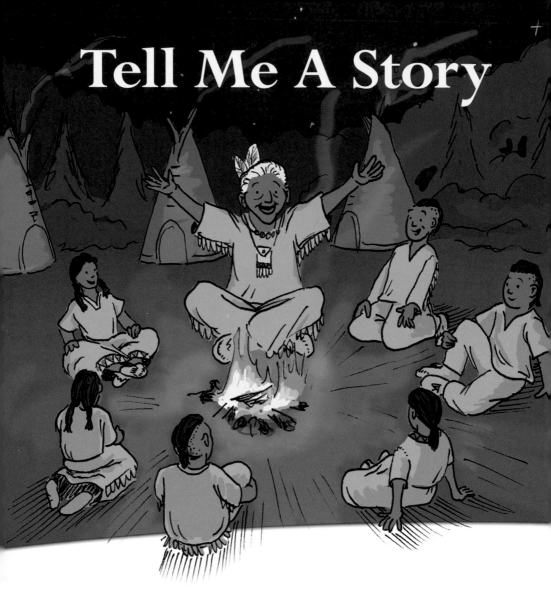

There were many groups of Native Americans. They lived all over America for thousands of years before the colonists arrived. Each had unique art, beliefs, stories, and ways of living their lives. Traditions were passed down **orally** by telling stories of their **ancestors**, beliefs and practices.

Grandparents taught children lessons by telling **Trickster Tales**. The trickster was usually a coyote that got into trouble. Colonial children learned similar lessons through **Aesop's Fables**. Kids today still enjoy these animal stories.

Glossary

ancestors: people from your family that lived before you.

Aesop's Fables: a collection of stories that teach a lesson, written by the Greek storyteller Aesop.

ball: a fancy party with dancing.

barn raising: building a wooden barn with a group of people.

beam: a strong piece of wood laid across posts for support.

bonds: links between people.

Colonial America: the name given to this country when talking about the years 1607–1776.

colonist: a person who came to settle America.

communicate: to exchange information or ideas.

community: a group of people living in an area together.

cornhusking: a party held to peel ears of corn.

culture: traditions of a group of people.

fine: money owed for breaking a law.

frolic: a planned work party or holiday gathering.

harpsichord: an instrument similar to a piano. It had an upper and lower keyboard.

harvest: the food grown on a farm.

hymns: songs written for praise or prayer.

New World: what settlers from Europe called America because it was new to them.

orally: spoken out loud.

Pilgrims: colonists who came from England in the 1620s to settle Massachusetts.

plantation: a large farm where crops are grown to sell.

post: a strong piece of wood stood straight up for support.

Puritans: a group of colonists that lived a simple life. Their religion was very strict.

recycle: to use something again.

slave: a person owned by another person and forced to work without pay.

traditions: ways of doing things for a group of people.

Trickster Tales: stories about an animal character that gets into trouble.

united: joined with others.

wadding: a layer of wool or cotton stuffing. It gives a quilt thickness and warmth.

Wampanoag: the Native American tribe that lived in the area where Massachusetts was founded.

Further Investigations

Books

Bordessa, Kris. *Great Colonial America Projects You Can Build Yourself.* White River Junction, VT: Nomad Press, 2006.

Fisher, Verna. *Explore Colonial America! 25 Great Projects, Activities, Experiments.* White River Junction, VT: Nomad Press, 2009.

Museums and Websites

Colonial Williamsburg
www.history.org
Williamsburg, Virginia

National Museum of the American Indian
www.nmai.si.edu
Washington, D.C. and
New York, New York

Plimoth Plantation
www.plimoth.org
Plymouth, Massachusetts

America's Library
www.americaslibrary.gov

Jamestown Settlement
www.historyisfun.org

Native American History
www.bigorrin.org

Native Languages of the Americas
www.native-languages.org

Social Studies for Kids
www.socialstudiesforkids.com

The Mayflower
www.mayflowerhistory.com

Virtual Jamestown
www.virtualjamestown.org

Index